FRANCIS FRITH'S

WHITBY

PHOTOGRAPHIC MEMORIES

CORDELIA STAMP has lived and worked in Whitby for almost fifty years. Whitby has always been a well-loved place in her affections; first in childhood years before the war and then, after war service in the army, as a home teacher of the blind. With her late husband, Tom, she founded the publishing firm Caedmon of Whitby, and together they wrote the biographies of two of Whitby's most famous sons, William Scoresby and James Cook.

FRANCIS FRITH'S
PHOTOGRAPHIC MEMORIES

WHITBY

PHOTOGRAPHIC MEMORIES

CORDELIA STAMP

First published in the United Kingdom in 2005

Limited hardback edition published in 2005
ISBN 1-84589-012-4

Paperback edition 2005
ISBN 1-85937-491-3

British Library Cataloguing in Publication Data

Whitby - Photographic Memories
Cordelia Stamp

The Francis Frith Collection
Frith's Barn, Teffont,
Salisbury, Wiltshire SP3 5QP
Tel: +44 (0) 1722 716 376
Email: info@francisfrith.co.uk
www.francisfrith.co.uk

Printed and bound in Great Britain

Front Cover: **WHITBY**, *The Quay 1927* 80177t
Frontispiece: **WHITBY**, *West Cliff 1901* 46788

*The colour-tinting is for illustrative purposes only, and is not intended to be
historically accurate*

Aerial photographs reproduced under licence from
Simmons Aerofilms Limited.
Historical Ordnance Survey maps reproduced under licence from
Homecheck.co.uk
Every attempt has been made to contact copyright holders of
illustrative material. We will be happy to give full acknowledge-
ment in future editions for any items not credited. Any informa-
tion should be directed to The Francis Frith Collection.

AS WITH ANY HISTORICAL DATABASE THE FRITH ARCHIVE IS CONSTANTLY
BEING CORRECTED AND IMPROVED AND THE PUBLISHERS WOULD WELCOME
INFORMATION ON OMISSIONS OR INACCURACIES

CONTENTS

FRANCIS FRITH
VICTORIAN PIONEER

FRANCIS FRITH, founder of the world-famous photographic archive, was a complex and multi-talented man. A devout Quaker and a highly successful Victorian businessman, he was philosophical by nature and pioneering in outlook.

By 1855 he had already established a wholesale grocery business in Liverpool, and sold it for the astonishing sum of £200,000, which is the equivalent today of over £15,000,000. Now a very rich man, he was able to indulge his passion for travel. As a child he had pored over travel books written by early explorers, and his fancy and imagination had been stirred by family holidays to the sublime mountain regions of Wales and Scotland. 'What lands of spirit-stirring and enriching scenes and places!' he had written. He was to return to these scenes of grandeur in later years to 'recapture the thousands of vivid and tender memories', but with a different purpose. Now in his thirties, and captivated by the new science of photography, Frith set out on a series of pioneering journeys up the Nile and to the

Near East that occupied him from 1856 until 1860.

INTRIGUE AND EXPLORATION

These far-flung journeys were packed with intrigue and adventure. In his life story, written when he was sixty-three, Frith tells of being held captive by bandits, and of fighting 'an awful midnight battle to the very point of surrender with a deadly pack of hungry, wild dogs'. Wearing flowing Arab costume, Frith arrived at Akaba by camel sixty years before Lawrence of Arabia, where he encountered 'desert princes and rival sheikhs, blazing with jewel-hilted swords'.

He was the first photographer to venture beyond the sixth cataract of the Nile. Africa was still the mysterious 'Dark Continent', and Stanley and Livingstone's historic meeting was a decade into the future. The conditions for picture taking confound belief. He laboured for hours in his wicker dark-room in the sweltering heat of the desert, while the volatile chemicals fizzed dangerously in their trays. Back in London he exhibited his photographs and was 'rapturously cheered' by members of the Royal Society. His reputation as a photographer was made overnight.

VENTURE OF A LIFE-TIME

Characteristically, Frith quickly spotted the opportunity to create a new business as a specialist publisher of photographs. He lived in an era of immense and sometimes violent change.

For the poor in the early part of Victoria's reign work was exhausting and the hours long, and people had precious little free time to enjoy themselves. Most had no transport other than a cart or gig at their disposal, and rarely travelled far beyond the boundaries of their own town or village. However, by the 1870s the railways had threaded their way across the country, and Bank Holidays and half-day Saturdays had been made obligatory by Act of Parliament. All of a sudden the working man and his family were able to enjoy days out and see a little more of the world.

With typical business acumen, Francis Frith foresaw that these new tourists would enjoy having souvenirs to commemorate their days out. In 1860 he married Mary Ann Rosling and set out on a new career: his aim was to photograph every city, town and village in Britain. For the next thirty years he travelled the country by train and by pony and trap, producing fine photographs of seaside resorts and beauty spots that were keenly bought by millions of Victorians. These prints were painstakingly pasted into family albums and pored over during the dark nights of winter, rekindling precious memories of summer excursions.

THE RISE OF FRITH & CO

Frith's studio was soon supplying retail shops all over the country. To meet the demand he gathered about him a small team of photographers, and published the work of independent artist-photographers of the calibre of Roger Fenton and Francis Bedford. In order to gain some understanding of the scale of Frith's business one only has to look at the catalogue issued by Frith & Co in 1886: it runs to some 670 pages, listing not only many thousands of views of the British Isles but also many photographs of most European countries, and China, Japan, the USA and Canada - note the sample page shown on page 9 from the hand-written Frith & Co ledgers recording the pictures. By 1890 Frith had created the greatest specialist photographic publishing company in the world, with over 2,000 sales outlets - more than the combined number that Boots and WH Smith have today! The picture on the next page shows the Frith & Co display board at Ingleton in the Yorkshire Dales (left of window). Beautifully constructed with a mahogany frame and gilt inserts, it could display up to a dozen local scenes.

POSTCARD BONANZA

The ever-popular holiday postcard we know today took many years to develop. In 1870 the Post Office issued the first plain cards, with a pre-printed stamp on one face. In 1894 they allowed other publishers' cards to be sent through the mail with an attached adhesive halfpenny stamp. Demand grew rapidly, and in 1895 a new size of postcard was permitted called the court card, but there was little room for illustration. In 1899, a year after Frith's death, a new card measuring 5.5 x 3.5 inches became the standard format, but it was not until 1902 that the divided back came into being, so that the address and message could be on one face and a full-size illustration on the other. Frith & Co were in the vanguard of postcard development: Frith's sons Eustace and Cyril continued their father's monumental task, expanding the number of views offered to the public and recording more and more places in Britain, as the coasts and countryside were opened up to mass travel.

Francis Frith had died in 1898 at his villa in Cannes, his great project still growing. The archive he created continued in business for another seventy years. By 1970 it contained over a third of a million pictures showing 7,000 British towns and villages.

FRANCIS FRITH'S LEGACY

Frith's legacy to us today is of immense significance and value, for the magnificent archive of evocative photographs he created provides a unique record of change in the cities, towns and villages throughout Britain over a century and more. Frith and his fellow studio photographers revisited locations many times down the years to update their views, compiling for us an enthralling and colourful pageant of British life and character.

We are fortunate that Frith was dedicated to recording the minutiae of everyday life. For it is this sheer wealth of visual data, the painstaking chronicle of changes in dress, transport, street layouts, buildings, housing, engineering and landscape that captivates us so much today. His remarkable images offer us a powerful link with the past and with the lives of our ancestors.

THE VALUE OF THE ARCHIVE TODAY

Computers have now made it possible for Frith's many thousands of images to be accessed almost instantly. Frith's images are increasingly used as visual resources, by social historians, by researchers into genealogy and ancestry, by architects and town planners, and by teachers involved in local history projects.

In addition, the archive offers every one of us an opportunity to examine the places where we and our families have lived and worked down the years. Highly successful in Frith's own era, the archive is now, a century and more on, entering a new phase of popularity. Historians consider the Francis Frith Collection to be of prime national importance. It is the only archive of its kind remaining in private ownership. Francis Frith's archive is now housed in an historic timber barn in the beautiful village of Teffont in Wiltshire. Its founder would not recognize the archive office as it is today. In place of the many thousands of dusty boxes containing glass plate negatives and an all-pervading odour of photographic chemicals, there are now ranks of computer screens. He would be amazed to watch his images travelling round the world at unimaginable speeds through internet lines.

The archive's future is both bright and exciting. Francis Frith, with his unshakeable belief in making photographs available to the greatest number of people, would undoubtedly approve of what is being done today with his lifetime's work. His photographs depicting our shared past are now bringing pleasure and enlightenment to millions around the world a century and more after his death.

WHITBY
AN INTRODUCTION

It is remarkable that the small seaport of Whitby, for centuries relatively isolated, does nevertheless hold a recognised place in the monastic and maritime history of our peoples. To have been the scene of the Synod of Whitby; to have nurtured Caedmon, the first English poet; to have fostered the genius of Cook, giving him his marriage certificate to the sea and building his ships; to have fathered the abilities of the Scoresbys and bred the hardy adventurous spirits that went with them to the Greenland seas ... these are no small claim to fame.

It was from this ancient seaport that Cook sailed, for it was here that he was turned from an inland youth to a man of the sea. The process began at Staithes among the fishing folk and their small craft, and at Whitby he was irrevocably wed to the sea.

All this slumbers in the past, only to be awakened by the occasional commemorative ceremonies. But Whitby does not live in the past, only thrives in it, for people come from all over the world to relish the romance of the past and find the Whitby of the present time. For Whitby binds us to herself, we folk who love her well.

This is not intended to be a factual historical account of the ancient foundations of this place. For that, the reader must search the history books. It is enough to say that the Romans were here, to which some of their remaining straight roads testify. Then came the Saxons, and Whitby was called Streonshalh at that time; I like to think that our present name derived from a white bay, but the purists will doubtless have other theories.

The Synod of Whitby

Most of our knowledge of those early days derives from the Venerable Bede, saint and scholar of the eighth century AD; he wrote a wonderful account in his 'The Ecclesiastical History of the English People', the single most valuable source for early English history, which he finished in 731. It is from him that we learn how St Hilda came from Hartlepool in the mid seventh century and founded the monastery whose fame, in six short years, spread far and wide. It was here in 664 that the Synod of Whitby was held to resolve the differences between Celtic and Roman Christianity, particularly over the date of Easter; following the synod, the English church was unified under the Roman discipline, and the date of the Easter festival was settled. Here, too, we are told, dwelt Caedmon, the first English poet. He was inspired to sing by a vision in which an angel appeared to him, and he told of the creation and God's world in song. When Hilda heard of his talent, she took him into the community, and he became a monk, for it was a mixed monastery of both nuns and monks.

The early primitive abbey buildings survived for a time, but after the mid eighth century, the abbey disappeared from the historical record. It was probably destroyed by the Viking invaders around 867. It was not until the 11th century that the stone abbey that is familiar to us today was begun by Norman Benedictine monks during the revival of monasticism in England. The abbey was altered and rebuilt over the years; most of what we see today dates from the 13th and early 14th centuries. Then the greed and rapacity of Henry VIII brought about the end of the monasteries – the last abbot of Whitby, Henry de Vall, was forced to surrender the abbey to Henry VIII's commissioners in December 1539.

In medieval times the town of Whitby was a snug collection of small houses clinging to the cliffs below the abbey; they were arranged in numerous yards, each of which was enclosed by a sturdy gate strong enough to repel any seaward invasion. As for roads, there were hardly any save narrow, stony tracks over the moors; almost all access was from the sea. A bridge was a late innovation, built in the 16th century - before then the river had to be crossed by fords. This bridge was a wooden drawbridge, rather Dutch in style; it was rebuilt in 1766, and demolished in 1835, to be replaced by a stone bridge. The present swing bridge dates from 1908, and the high level bridge further up river was opened in 1980 to allow traffic to bypass the town.

The first inhabitants of Whitby made their living in the first instance under the patronage of the abbey, working on the abbey's farms and buildings as shepherds, herdsmen, joiners, masons, and labourers, and as lay brothers and sisters, serving the abbey under vows of chastity and obedience, but exempt from the studies and duties of monks and nuns. The fishing trade developed gradually. From the Middle Ages

WHITBY ABBEY *1901* 46790

onwards the prosperity of Whitby was largely derived from fishing; large seasonal catches of herring could be made along this coast. So the town grew, and the original medieval East Cliff started to extend upwards and outwards and across the river to the west cliff.

Whitby has always been a busy trading port. In the 16th century, alum was the main cargo, and in the 17th and 18th centuries, coal was shipped to and from Tyneside, and the ship building industry began. In 1706, Whitby was the sixth most important port in Britain, building 130 ships a year. The great days of whaling lasted from about 1735 to the early years of the 19th century – the loss of the whaling ships 'Lively' and 'Esk' in 1826 heralded the end of the whaling boom. During the 19th century Whitby was an important herring fishing centre. The fishermen built their own boats, and large cargo vessels continued to be built in the shipyards until 1908. Today, fishing boats, mainly Yorkshire cobles, are built at two small yards, and trading continues – Whitby imports and exports timber, limestone, paper, and steel products.

A word about east and west. One might logically think that the site of the abbey and the old town lies south of the river Esk and that the comparatively more recent buildings of Whitby lie on the north side. Not so. Thanks to an odd twist of the coastline, Whitby actually faces north, and so in midsummer we can watch the sun setting in the sea. Thus it is that the cliffs either side of the river are respectively west and east.

Georgian Times

Before the age of steam, ships were generally on the small side, and Whitby's harbour could accommodate them. During the reigns of the Georges, the town began to spread out. Her new-found wealth came from the expansion of the shipping trade, both in the whaling industry and maritime commerce. Thus it came about that wealthy ship owners were able to build their stately houses, mansions and even estates.

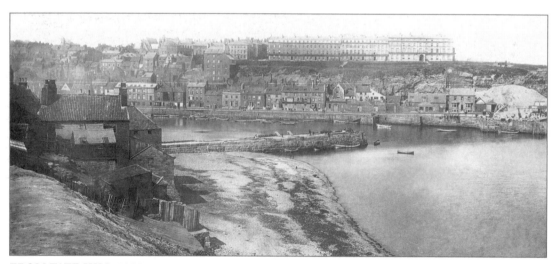

FROM TATE HILL *1885* 18164

Retail trade had also expanded, and shop-keepers and tradesmen were quick to take advantage of the new boom. Some 52 grocers and 30 drapers are listed by George Young, the famous historian, in his 'History of Whitby' of 1817. He also lists numerous masons and brick-layers, glaziers, hatters and hairdressers, ship chandlers and victuallers. At this time, he tells us, the town contained 7 jewellers' shops, 6 hardware shops, 6 toy shops and 6 slop shops (a slop shop sold ready-made clothes); dealers in ale and porter amount to 65 and in tea 72, but it appears that the 83 dealers in tobacco exceed the others.

The Collector of Customs was kept busy, and he had over a score of various helpers to assist him in detecting smuggling activity. The average number of ships bringing their cargo to Whitby was around 370 during the time of Waterloo, whilst many more ships sheltered in the port during stormy weather. We are told by George Young that 'the revenue of the Custom House varies greatly according to circumstances, but the average sum may be stated at less than £900'.

Local Heroes

Captain James Cook, the famous navigator, surveyor and sea captain, must be the most celebrated figure associated with Whitby. Born in Marton in 1728, he worked in a haberdasher's at Staithes, and then came to Whitby, where he was apprenticed to a ship owner. He spent some years in the coasting and Baltic trade, and then joined the Navy, where he rose through the ranks, becoming master in 1759. He displayed exceptional ability as a navigator and surveyor, and in 1768, after surveying the St Lawrence and the Newfoundland coast, he commanded the 'Endeavour' for the Royal Society expedition to the Pacific. This was the first of his three major expeditions, in each of which he sailed in boats built in Whitby, including the 'Resolution'. He also worked out how to prevent scurvy. His last voyage was to discover a passage round the north coast of America from the Pacific, but he was forced to turn back in the Bering Strait, reaching Hawaii in 1779. Here he was killed at the age of fifty. His statue overlooks Whitby harbour.

THE FISH QUAY *1923* 74318

The Scoresbys, father and son, deserve greater fame. William Scoresby senior, inventor of the crow's nest, was born in 1760 south of Whitby; he was apprenticed to a Whitby shipowner and served on whaling ships. He rapidly worked his way up to command a Greenland whaler, the 'Henrietta', in 1790, and the 'Dundee' in 1798, and was remarkably successful, catching 80 whales between 1792 and 1797. He formed a partnership to build a new Greenland whaler, 'Resolution', launched in 1803; in 1810 he formed the Greenock Whale and Fishing Company with three Greenock businessmen. His whaling exploits were finally ended when his ship 'Fame' was destroyed by fire in the Orkneys. His retirement years were devoted to improvements for Whitby, including suggestions for lengthening the piers. He died in 1829.

William junior's fame rests on his achievements as an explorer and scientist. Born in 1789, he served as a boy on his father's whaling ships. He went to Edinburgh University, where he studied chemistry and physics. After a spell in command of his father's whaler the 'Resolution', he commanded the 'Esk', in which he explored Arctic seas and lands and carried out experiments on the temperature of the sea. In 1806 the two Scoresbys attained a Furthest North record, reaching 81°30 north, the nearest approach to the North Pole ever made by sailing ship. In 1820 William junior published 'An Account of the Arctic Regions', the first scientific account of the area, and in 1822 he surveyed 400 miles of the Greenland coast. In 1825 he was ordained, but he continued with his scientific investigations. In 1838 he was asked by the Admiralty to assist with the construction of compass needles. Shortly before his death in 1857, he sailed to Australia to study terrestrial magnetism.

Victorian Development

The coming of the railway in the 1830s changed the entire face of the town, bringing visitors from far afield. The property developers of those Victorian days pushed up more and more boarding houses to accommodate the new influx. Chief among these was George Hudson, the railway king. Born in Yorkshire in 1800, he used a legacy to buy railway shares, which started him off on his headlong career of investing in the railways and forming railway companies. At the height of his success in the early 1840s, he and his companies controlled over a thousand miles of railway track, and he was worth hundreds of thousands of pounds. At one point he was friendly with Stephenson, the railway engineer, and with the Duke of Wellington, whom he advised on share dealing. He dominated the greater part of Whitby's West Cliff with his property development schemes, even intending to out-do Bath and its famous Crescent. Alas! Before he could complete Royal Crescent, his money and his fame ran out. So today we have to be content with only half of his original ambitious design.

Long tradition has meant that employment is sought by the menfolk, who have had to work away from the town, first of all by going to sea, and latterly in nearby developing industries, largely in Teesside but also on oil rigs in oceanic isolation. This has meant that over the years the womenfolk have been left to run their homes, families and even the town. The matriarchal tradition remains.

Another old tradition is not now so widespread. The sea-going fraternity endeavoured to invest their hard-earned savings in houses bought in their wife's name so that she would have an income should they be drowned, a not uncommon event then; this was a prudent precaution in the days before the welfare state.

Whitby Jet

Whitby owes much to Queen Victoria. She it was who went spectacularly into permanent mourning after the death of her husband, Prince Albert, and all was black thereafter – she had made the outward show of sorrow fashionable. The town's jet industry came into its own. Jet craftsmen appeared all over Whitby working on this fossilised Araucaria - or Monkey Puzzle tree, if you prefer. It was fortunate that in very ancient days, twenty million years or so ago, there must have been a forest of these trees around this area, for Whitby's is one of the best deposits anywhere in the world. Local men were not slow to start digging up the black gold all along the coastal area. Jet lends itself to intricate carving and a high polish, and a local man, Captain Tremlett, invented a way of turning jet to make beads. Thus, thanks to new technology (there was at least one gas-powered lathe in Whitby at one point) and interest from the royal family, jet trinkets became desirable. In the 1870s, about 1400 men and boys were employed in the industry. However, by the 1930s it had dwindled drastically, although it is still possible to buy jet jewellery in Whitby shops today. There are some wonderful examples of the jet craftsmen's skill in the museum.

Whitby's Later History

Not so very long ago, access to the town was a simple matter for rail travellers. Not only did the LNER provide excursion trains for day trips, but it also

JET WORKERS *1890* ZZZ02103 *(Reproduced by kind permission of the Sutcliffe Gallery)*
It is unlikely that Frank Sutcliffe knew he was photographing a bit of history when he took this picture, but so it has turned out. He was, of course, the renowned Whitby photographer; born in 1853, from the 1880s he made photographic studies of the vanishing world of the farm workers and particularly the fishermen of Yorkshire. He also supplied photographs to Francis Frith's company at one time. From the late 1890s he used the new lightweight cameras, and was thus able to capture spontaneous moments. He retired in 1923 and died in 1941.

brought hundreds of city dwellers to stay here for a length of time. Many families spent their summer holidays in the resort, taking the children to the beach daily – for in our youth, did not the sun shine every day? In the rare event of bad weather, they could seek the shelter of the Spa complex.

Then along came the fell hand of Dr Beeching and his ill-advised axe. No more trains direct from York. Instead, the bemused traveller is routed further north by an extra ninety miles or so in order to visit this well loved spot.

There have been constant attempts by know-all construction firms wishing to line their own pockets by demolishing some of the existing buildings and putting in their place very dubious 'developments'. Despite the almost total resistance to their plans, I am sorry to say that a few monstrosities have already slipped through the net. However, as this book is about our town's earlier days, I shall say no more, but leave the reader to form his or her own opinion.

A translation of the words on our coat of arms, 'Fuimus et Sumus', would read: 'We have been and we are'.

WHITBY COAT OF ARMS ZZZ02409
Reproduced by kind permission of Whitby Borough Council

THE ABBEY,
THE PARISH CHURCH,
ABBEY HOUSE AND
CHURCH STAIRS

WHITBY ABBEY *1901* 46790
'They dreamt not of a perishable home who thus could build'.
(Tennyson)

WHITBY FROM THE AIR *1965* AFA152957

THE PARISH CHURCH *1913* 66278

When the visitors finished climbing the 199 church steps, they encountered the Caedmon Cross at the top. It is a replica of the ancient Ruthwell Cross, and was placed here in 1892 by the efforts of Canon Rawnsley, one of the founders of the National Trust. The parish church is Norman in origin, but has been much altered and enlarged over the centuries; its interior is remarkably idiosyncratic and attractive.

THE PARISH CHURCH FROM THE ABBEY *1913* 66279

This charming vignette seen through the old abbey ruins also manages to give us an insight into the sadly neglected state of this historic building with its grass-grown walls before it was taken over by the Ministry of Works, later known as English Heritage.

WHITBY ABBEY ARCHES *1913* 66281

This photograph shows a very different picture from today's carefully mown and tended lawns. Once the lead had been removed from the roof it was not long before the structure began to crumble, and many of the stones were taken. Here and there a few monastic stones can be found in some Whitby walls and buildings. The west front largely collapsed in 1914 after a raid by German battle cruisers, which shelled Whitby and scored a hit on the abbey. The façade has since been partially rebuilt.

21

CHURCH STEPS *1913* 66284

It is thought that the church steps were originally built in the early 14th century to enable access to the church from the old town, and at that time the steps were wooden, not stone. The steps we see today are about 200 years old, and were probably built by local and itinerant labourers. Coffins were carried up the steps to the church, and there are still 'coffin rests' to be seen here. A red light on the steps warns vessels if they are approaching harbour on an unsafe bearing. Hobble skirts, although the height of fashion, were not designed for climbing steps. The little girl looks as if she might be counting the steps on the way down, just to be sure there were 199 on the way up!

THE PARISH CHURCH
The Gallery Entrance 1913
66287

The churchwarden awaits the arrival of the owners of the abbey (who at this date would have been the Stricklands), ready to escort them up to their private gallery in the church; the gallery was built in the early 17th century by the Cholmleys, who had owned the abbey since the Dissolution. The churchwarden stands by the Huntrods tomb, which is remarkable for its recording of the identical ages of the birth and death of the Huntrods couple.

ABBEY HOUSE *1901* ZZZ02099 *(Reproduced by kind permission of Whitby Archives)*

This was the one-time home of the Cholmley family. Richard Cholmley, 'the great black knight of the North', leased and later bought the abbey after the dissolution. His son Francis remodelled the old abbot's lodging and used it as his house. Sir Hugh Cholmley improved Abbey House in the 1630s, and his son, also Hugh, built an impressive classical-style range in front of the older building in 1672 – unfortunately, it fell into decay after the loss of its roof in the 1790s. In 1866 the house was again extended by W C Strickland (it is this extension we see in the photograph); it was later run by the Co-operative Holiday Association as a holiday hotel. A new Visitor Centre was constructed inside the restored Cholmley range in 2002.

SUMMER HOLIDAYS
1899 ZZZ02100
(Reproduced by kind permission of Whitby Archives)

This group photograph of happy holidaymakers at the Co-operative Holiday Association's holiday hotel at Abbey House poses many questions. Firstly, the absence of children suggests a preponderance of single women. Secondly, if they are all from Co-op shops, then who is looking after the customers meanwhile? There are a good many older women in the group; one wonders if they were retired Co-op shop assistants. What do you think?

EAST CLIFF, CHURCH STREET, THE YARDS

FROM SPRING HILL *1885* 18166

This interesting view was taken from the western side of
the river from the site of today's police station, and shows
many of the yards along Church Street. The topmost
block of seven houses is appropriately named Elbow Yard.
St Michael's Church, demolished in the next century to
make room for a car park, can be seen in the centre.
At this time Church Street and its environs had a large
resident population (which moved in the ensuing century
to Helredale, the council estate), which provided both a
congregation for the church and pupils for its school.

EAST CLIFF
1901 46779

The picturesque cottages of the east side surround the 199 church stairs. This was probably a Monday, as the washing is laid to dry on the sands. The square building to the left of the bridge is the old Market Hall which later became Town Tailors and then Burberrys, both providing welcome employment locally.

EAST CLIFF *1913* 66263

On the extreme left we can just see the so-called Spa ladder, leading to the East Pier. On the right side we can see the back of the Cholmley School, which was endowed by Lady Cholmley in 1869. The building is still used today as the headquarters of a rowing club. The large building behind was the Methodist chapel, since demolished.

▼ **EAST CLIFF** *1923* 74310

This panoramic view of Henrietta Street and East Cliff was probably taken from the West Pier extension. The lighthouse there was built in 1831 from the design of Francis Pickernell, the Engineer to the Harbour Trustees; it is worked manually, and is used only when vessels are expected. Its green light has a range of ten miles. It is 83 feet tall, and open to the public – there is a fine view from the top. The smaller lighthouse on the East Pier (54 feet tall) was erected in 1854. The lighthouses were essential to guide ships safely to harbour; this rocky coast has claimed many victims. Whitby has had numerous lifeboats; among many heroic rescue attempts, perhaps the most tragic was in 1861, when only one of the lifeboat crew, Henry Freeman, escaped death – he was wearing a newly-invented cork lifejacket.

▶ **THE VIEW FROM THE COOK STATUE** *1932* 85340

And if you still don't believe that Whitby faces north, just look on top of the flagpole. It is a long climb to this point up from the quayside, though not quite as high as the Church Steps.

◄ EAST CLIFF
1932 85342

The donkeys have a long walk every day from their field just below the Abbey House, down the donkey path, along Church Street, over the bridge and down Pier Road to the sands. It is washday again; this time the linen is pegged on a line on Tate Hill sands. Washing machines were almost unknown at this date, and owned only by rich people. As for automatic dryers, they lay only in the future. Old deeds of many of the East Cliff houses often included particulars of 'drying grounds', the rights of which came with the building in question. The concerned housewives often settled the problem between themselves as to which days 'their' portion of the drying ground might be available.

► THE VIEW FROM THE CAR PARK
c1955 W81035

One sees so many small things in old photographs that one simply took for granted at the time. Today, how often do we see men walking along arm in arm? The old 'charas' now graced by the name of coaches brought many day trippers to our old port. This picture gives a good view of St Michael's Church, which was demolished some ten years later.

'GEMINI'
1891 28862

These two children have provoked much speculation in the town today. Girls or boys? East side or west side? Twins or not? After the Whitby Gazette was kind enough to publish their picture, we received help from several sources. We can now state that they are certainly boys and, as the title indicates, twins. Best of all, we found a great-great-grandson of Matthew Peart (left) living in Whitby today, Geoffrey Vasey. The other three-year-old is Robert Peart (right); his life was short, as he was tragically drowned at the age of twenty when he was swept overboard near St Petersburg.

STUDY OF CHILDREN
1891 28867

Here we see Robert Peart and his sister Jennie, who was six, on the rocks below their home on Tate Hill Pier. Michael Yates identified them; he relates that Jennie, named after her mother Jane Peart (nee Leadley), later became Mrs Swales.

A GROUP OF FISHER CHILDREN *1891* 28866

The Pearts' eldest daughter Amelia (17) holds her baby brother, George; the twins take a rather damp seat on the seaweedy rock, and Jennie and Tom watch the photographer put them all in the frame for posterity. Michael Yates's wife Marion tells us that Amelia later married Tom Eglon, one of her relatives.

ARGUMENTS YARD *1913* 66290

We can clearly see the derelict state of this particular yard in Church Street. Although it was a favourite subject for artists and photographers, they could hardly have known how difficult life must have been for the inhabitants, these barefoot boys amongst them.

TIN GHAUT *1913* 66292

A ghaut (a Viking word) is a narrow passage leading to the river. There used to be an inn at the end of this one, so in the local dialect it became known as T'inn Ghaut. It was deemed picturesque by artists and photographers, but life was hard here. Providing boots and shoes for the children was a major problem for parents, and there was a special charity for this purpose to assist them. It is not surprising that a place renowned for fishing should have a large feline population, for there would always be enough fish scraps to feed them.

LOGGERHEAD YARD *1899* ZZZ02101 *(Reproduced by kind permission of Whitby Archives)*

An indoor piped water supply was not universal at this time; here we see a mother drawing the family water supply from a communal tap in the yard.

THE HARBOUR, THE BRIDGE, ST ANN'S STAITH, PIER ROAD, THE FISH MARKET, THE PIERS

ST ANN'S STAITH *1886* 18167

By now the advent of steam was apparent even in small craft. Looming on the skyline is the back of the Streonshalh Hotel; one can appreciate the extensive view that the hotel guests would have had. The second shop from the left is T E Clegg's shoe shop; how many fisher families could have afforded shoes?

THE HARBOUR
1885 18168

The Dock End has yet to be cleared out and made into a safe haven for the fishing fleet boats in bad weather. This last can be seen seventy years later in the picture of the railway station (W81011, p70). Behind the schooner 'Astrea' we can just see the Angel Vaults; the Angel Hotel was an old coaching inn. A close-up examination of the photograph reveals that one of the buildings in the background on the right was Harker's Wholesale Jet Ornament Manufactory.

THE LOWER HARBOUR *1891* 28854

Whitby harbour was renowned for its narrow entry between the two piers with their lighthouses. The whaling ships had to wait for the high tides to carry them through safely. The little fishing cobles had no problems, provided the wind was in the right quarter. A coble (pronounced 'cobble') is a very ancient type of fishing boat that goes back to Viking times. It is clinker built, with a flat bottom for landing on the beach.

▶ **MARINE PARADE**
1955 W81038

Little has changed over the years since the 1950s. Then as now, one could dawdle on the way to the beach and look at the gift shops or stop for a cuppa, or even have some oysters – an oyster stall is just visible (centre left). Dorans the photographers sold their pictures here, and further on, in the middle of Pier Road, there was the Magpie Café, still today nationally famous for fish and chips. A long queue stretches outside the café during the holiday season.

◄ THE UPPER HARBOUR
1955 W81040

Directly above St Michael's Church (right) one can see Abbey House and the ruined shell of the classical banqueting hall built by Sir Hugh Cholmley in 1672, roofless since the 1790s; at the time of this photograph, it was in the care of the Ministry of Works. It was taken over this century by English Heritage; they now call the site the Headland, but local people prefer to continue calling it the Abbey Plain. Tin Ghaut and the adjoining houses up to the church have now been demolished to make room for a car park. It is called Progress ... but I wonder.

THE FISH QUAY
1923 74318

Here we see the early morning scene at the fish market after the catch has been landed and sorted. The auctioneer is at the far end. For a very long time Whitby did not have such a thing as a fish shop, as the fishermen themselves supplied their wives, and most locals bought their fish from Jack Gash and his barrow.

▶ **THE FISH QUAY**
1927 80177

The crowd look on as the catch is being landed for the market. An expectant bevy of seagulls watch carefully in case there are any fishy morsels coming in their direction. Years ago, the quay would have been bustling with women gutting the herring and packing them into barrels with salt and ice. Today, the local fleet is a tiny one in comparison with the fleet of 100 years ago, the fish they catch, like the herring of yore, may well be transported far away before it is eaten.

◀ **WATCHING THE FISHING FLEET**
1955 W81148

Half the pleasure of being on holiday oneself is watching others working, and it certainly was hard work for the fishermen off-loading their catch at the market.
The Friendship Rowing club have moved their pontoon down river from their previous anchorage, as seen in 87334 on page 46.

◢ THE PIER *1891* 28857

If the railway viaduct carrying the LNER from Teeside to Scarborough is a memorial to its bricklayers, then how much more should the two piers at the harbour mouth be a tribute to those men of stone, the engineers and masons who first built them. They knew their job, for they built them to withstand the tremendous force of storm winds and tides. And still they stand. It is uncertain how old the piers are; the first mention of them is in Henry VIII's time. An act was passed in 1709 to repair them.

◀ THE NEW PIER EXTENSIONS *1913*
66265a

There was great rejoicing when the new stone and iron extensions were finally erected in 1912, having first been suggested by William Scoresby the elder (1760-1829) a hundred years before. The extensions effectively enlarged the harbour entrance, making it safer for vessels to enter harbour in rough weather. The competent engineers left a space for turbulent seas to break through and lessen the strain on the masonry.

▼ THE PIERS *1927* 80178

When it is high tide the visitors can get their fresh sea air from the safety of Battery Parade. One intrepid youngster braves the waves. The pier extensions were constructed with the aid of the 'walking man', a huge metal scaffolding contraption that moved along the seabed to enable the building process. A foghorn on the west extension gives a blast every thirty seconds when visibility is poor.

► THE PIER
1955 W81152

Many of the people seen here would be day trippers rather than resident visitors, having come for a breath of fresh sea air on one of the many excursion trains from inland. At the time the pier extensions were constructed, some locals claimed that they had been built in the wrong direction, giving boats a rough passage over the harbour bar.

◀**THE BRIDGE**
1901 46788

The swivel section of the stone bridge built in 1835 to replace the old Dutch-style drawbridge opens to let a ship through. Then, as now, crowds gathered to watch the operation.

▶ **THE BRIDGE**
1913 66266

The new bridge, which was completed in 1908, was welcomed by pedestrians and ships alike. Its two sections span 75 feet; each section can be operated independently, swinging horizontally. The bridge is electrically operated. It is manned for two hours on either side of high water, and vessels request opening by radio. It was to be another sixty years or so before a second, high-level bridge was built farther up the river and eased the traffic congestion problem.

THE BRIDGE
1923 74316

If you should ask how the fishermen reached their cobles moored in the river, notice the steps (not to mention the mooring ropes). Boots Corner was a well-known landmark; the buildings demolished in 1975 included Boots, the Yorkshire Bank and Whitby Fish Sales. Woolworths had not then been built. Behind Boots Corner was another Corner where an intriguing notice read FISHING FOR CHILDREN ONLY.

NEW QUAY ROAD *1936* 87334

By this time the fishing boats were growing larger, but no trawlers had yet appeared. The Angel Hotel, an old coaching inn, can be seen on the left, and Collier's hardware store stands beside the bridge. In those days before people worried about pollution, most of the buildings were blackened by the continual shroud of coal smoke from domestic chimneys. Even the strongest sea winds could not cure that.

BRIDGE END
c1955 W81030

Boots Corner was quite a landmark, and there are still old customers around who preferred the old rather than the new shop in Baxtergate. There are no traffic lights here yet - it was to be another ten years before they appeared. Life was simpler for learner drivers then.

THE BRIDGE *c1955* W81121

The building on the right of the bridge was called the Custom House Hotel at this date - it was later named the Dolphin. The original Custom House was in Sandgate on the other side of the road. We can see the back of the old Co-op - it is the building with the white gable end to the left. Workmen are putting the finishing touches to the new Cartridge's roof.

SAILING FROM THE HARBOUR
1955 W81147

By this time the humble fishing cobles had developed into a sizeable fishing fleet of much larger boats, which meant that they could travel further afield for their catch.
At the time of the herring fleet's arrival from Scotland, the boats completely filled the harbour, and it used to be said that one could walk right across the river without using the bridge.

WEST CLIFF - KHYBER PASS, THE ROYAL HOTEL, THE METROPOLE, THE SPA, ROYAL CRESCENT, THE PARK, THE MUSEUM

FROM TATE HILL *1885* 18164

Taken long before the days of amusement arcades and the bandstand, this photograph shows that Pier Road and the Crag consisted solely of dwelling houses, probably occupied mainly by the fishing community. Above them the newly built Royal Hotel (right) and Kirby's Hotel, erected to accommodate the growing number of visitors, dominate West Cliff. On the extreme right we can see the start of the building of Khyber Pass, the new road leading up West Cliff.

50

WEST CLIFF
1891 28852

The low tide has left a good deal of Tate Hill sands uncovered. Since this photograph was taken in the summer time, there is not as much smoke coming from the dwelling houses along the Crag (which lies behind the houses on the river front), but there is still enough to show that dinner was being cooked. The spire of the Congregational church, locally known as 'the Congo', is just visible on the horizon to the left.

WEST CLIFF *1891* 28858

The bathing machines wait for customers on Scotch Head (right), and so do the stalls along Pier Road (centre). Were they selling seafood? The tide is out, but that does not stop the children having a paddle by Tate Hill Pier, which juts out in the foreground.

► **WEST CLIFF AND THE METROPOLE HOTEL**
1923 74297

The Metropole Hotel was one of the first in Whitby to have electric light; its glowing windows were a landmark for ships. After the Great War the holiday trade was resumed, and summer time saw the arrival of visitors with their young families. If the beach was too far afield for the older generation, then there were plenty of seats and shelters along the clifftop where one could sit in the sun or the shade, and catch up with the news in the Yorkshire Post or the Whitby Gazette. Notice the changing tents on the beach below (right).

► *(far right) detail from* 74297

◄ **THE METROPOLE HOTEL** *1923* 74300

The Spa can be seen on the left, but the familiar cliff paths had not been made at this time - it would have been more easily accessible from Royal Crescent, developed by George Hudson. The chimneys of Royal Cresent can be seen in the distance.

▶ WEST CLIFF
c1965 W81132

Kirby's Hotel was at the other end of the Royal Hotel, beyond that we can just see South Terrace. The oyster stall is at the start of Pier Road, the Magpie café is in the centre and amusement arcades have started to appear towards its end. Some of the Crag houses can be seen behind. The big building by the harbour is Slaters, who exported many cargoes of lime at that time. Whitby was rather at a crossroads position at that period, unsure whether her main income was to be harbour trade or tourism. The lime shipments caused a great deal of dust blowing about and Slaters were made to put up the large shed which is shown in this photograph. Forty years on, it appears that tourism has proved to be a more profitable source of income for the town.

◀ CAPTAIN COOK'S MONUMENT
1913 66270

Designed by John Tweed, the statue was presented to the town of Whitby by Gervase Beckett MP in 1912. It stands on West Cliff. Cook has a map in one hand and dividers in the other, and as the sculptor intended, he looks out to sea, his eyes on the distant horizon. The cannon in the background (to the left of the statue) was later moved to East Crescent.

▲ **KHYBER PASS** *1913* 66271

This road up from the beach was first started at the time that George Hudson bought the West Cliff Estate in the 1850s, and it got the name from the strategic pass important in the Afghan wars, which raged on and off for a large part of the 19th century. Whitby has long been addicted to giving nicknames both to people and places, and often the names stick. The Royal Hotel stands on the left.

◄**THE TWO PIERS**
1923 74311

This photograph was taken from the path below Captain Cook's statue leading to the downward steps. It shows the flagstaff with Cook's ship 'Resolution' on top. It is sad to see so many pictures of this era showing a preponderance of women, following the loss of so many men in the Great War which finished five years before.

◄ **KHYBER PASS AND THE HARBOUR**
1955 W81137

The large central building used to be the coastguard station, and the half-moon battery at its front is now provided with seats instead of guns, making it a favourite place to relax, whilst the building is now a popular cafe.

◄ **THE KHYBER PASS** *1925*
78977

The thing which is most striking about these old photographs is the absence of traffic. Just you try walking up Khyber Pass in the middle of the road today. The old coastguard building has been turned into a cafe. The steps lead up to West Cliff with the flagstaff and Cook's statue.

▲ **THE SUNKEN GARDENS,** *West Cliff 1923* 74304

Just sufficiently sheltered from the cruel east wind, the plants here flourished, and the parks department of the local council were rightly proud of the attractive way in which they bloomed throughout the holiday season in these and other flowerbeds along West Cliff. Today, I am sorry to say, this is a favourite site for skateboarders.

◄ **THE ROYAL HOTEL** *1925* 77722

By this date the Royal Hotel has a new glassed-in porch, and now guests can enjoy the fresh sea air without the north-east wind's assistance. Although the hotel provided employment for many local people, it used to be only in the summer months. Fairly recently, however, the hotel has been taken over by a very active travel company which also runs its own transport system, and it brings guests here all the year round.

► **CRESCENT TERRACE**
1925 78978

Beyond Crescent Terrace lies the Royal Hotel corner, which is in North Terrace. Bram Stoker, the author of 'Dracula', stayed in Royal Crescent in 1890; he imagined his heroine, Mina, running after the sleep-walking Lucy as she went 'along North Terrace and down the steps to the quayside', and thence to the abbey, where there was an encounter with a bat-like figure. The only thing about the story which is real is this picture of North Terrace.

► *(far right) detail from* 78978

◄ ROYAL CRESCENT
1923 74307

Here we see the first half of George Hudson's dream of outdoing Bath. The house where Bram Stoker stayed in 1890 is in the centre behind the lamppost. It was there that he started to write his most famous book, 'Dracula', setting much of it in Whitby. Alas! Before the crescent could be completed Hudson's fame and his money ran out. Today we have to be content with only half of his original ambitious design.

WEST CLIFF AND THE GARDENS *1934* 86123

This was to be the site of the other half of George Hudson's dream crescent; because of his bankruptcy, it stayed empty for a long time. Eventually the West Cliff Hotel appeared, and the Princess Royal Hotel (right) was built here half a century later in the 1920s. The Princess Royal became an old people's home, and has recently been converted into individual apartments. A reconverted omnibus, very similar to the one shown here (right), still goes the rounds of the town as a popular attraction for visitors.

PANNETT PARK *1932* 85344

A green lung in the centre of the town, the park was given to Whitby by Alderman Pannett. Formerly it was an orchard, and one or two fruit trees can still be found here and there, much to the delight of the scrumpers. The flowerbeds are carefully maintained by the council.

PANNETT PARK ART GALLERY
1932 85345

Art exhibitions are held regularly here, displaying local artists' work. The Town Council has its office here, and it also contains Whitby Museum, renowned for its collection of extant fossils, which is run by the Literary and Philosophy Society, colloquially known as the Lit and Phil. It is a dignified building; as are the Georgian houses of St Hilda's Terrace, some of which can be seen in the background.

PANNETT PARK *1934* 86130

The attractive lily pond makes a quiet haven where one can escape the busy world for a while and shelter, if need be, from the odd shower or strong sunshine.

THE SPA
1927 80171

The Spa was built in the Victorian era, when Whitby was hoping to become a second Bath. There was a theatre (built in 1878) in the large brick building, whilst its extension, the Floral Pavilion, had a glass roof. Its veranda was a favourite place for summer visitors to assemble, and in cooler weather there were concerts and tea dances indoors.

THE SPA AND THE PIER EXTENSIONS *1925* 77715

Here we see the well-loved old glass-roofed Floral Pavilion with the Spa Theatre behind. Then, as now, one could approach them from the drive at the front, but the zigzag paths also made access to the sands easier. The afternoon tea dances held here were very popular, and visitors could dance in the flower-filled pavilion below its clusters of hanging baskets. The Palm Court was well named, and the Parks Department were rightly proud of their showpiece.

THE GUINNESS CLOCK *1955* W81085

This wonderful Heath Robinson-like piece of horological fantasy made a tour of seaside resorts in the l950s. I took some of my blind friends to 'see' it, and they were allowed to touch it as well as to hear the extraordinary sounds it produced thanks to its striking mechanism.

THE TOWN - BAXTERGATE, SKINNER STREET, EAST CRESCENT, THE STATION, STRENSHALH, ST ANN'S AGAIN

BAXTERGATE *1923* 74309

Poop poop! Mr Toad might drive in just such a car! This was the older of Whitby's two shopping streets. Puckrin's chemist's shop (the white building on the right) stood for a further forty years. The bell tower of St Ninian's Church is just visible in the centre, and the nun on the left could well have been from either of the two convents in the town.

THE STREONSHALH HOTEL
1925 78979

This impressive building stands at the top of the Khyber Pass; it was later turned into flats. We can imagine its view of East Cliff and the harbour when we look at its back view in picture 18164 (page 50). The solidified bag of cement on the edge of the garden wall can still be seen today on the left-hand side, almost obscured by bushes.

EAST CRESCENT *1925* 78980

Rumour and gossip are not always to be relied upon. This is true in two cases about this early Victorian crescent. For a long time some residents there claimed that their house was the original Dracula location. It was not. Stoker stayed at 6 Royal Crescent. As for the cannon (right), it was put there after the Great War and by the Second World War it had gone. Rumour said it had been buried for security. People dug for it without avail. What is more likely is that it was taken at the time when the country needed scrap iron for munitions.

CHURCH STREET *1925* 78982

Demolition took its toll on the left side of this picture. On the opposite side we may identify the corner building and the Friends Meeting House; between them is one of the oldest houses in Whitby, certainly Tudor, possibly much older. In Tudor times, its roof was thatched. In case of fire, there were very long rakes which could remove the burning roof.

SKINNER STREET
1930 W81002

The Georgian house on the right is interesting. It is probably the last of the dwelling houses here, as most of them are now shops. It used to have a press gang hide-away cupboard upstairs. We can just see the cupola of Harold Mansions, an Edwardian apartment house, at the end of the street.

ST ANN'S STAITH *1913* 66267

In the year before the Great War the women still wore long skirts; notice the two mothers on the left with their children in go chairs, the ancestors of today's buggies. The Red Lion (third from the left) and the tobacconist's shop to its left later made way for the new Woolworths. Further on is the Buck Hotel, and further still is the Ship Inn.

▶ **FROM BOGHALL**
1886 18165

This photograph demonstrates clearly that the River Esk is tidal, for it shows vessels lying on the river bed at low tide. The collection of houses on the left were built after the advent of the railway in the 1830s, and though named Fishburn Park, in honour of the local ship building family, they are known locally as 'The Railway'.

◄ **WHITBY FROM LARPOOL**
1881   14465

With a little stretch of the imagination one can visualise the original medieval town huddled below the abbey and the church. The entire left bank in the picture would then have been uncultivated land.

◄ *(far left) detail from* 14465

**DOCK END
AND THE
STATION**
1955 W81011

The dredging and
reclamation of this
part of the river was
short lived, and
today it has been
turned into car
parking space.
The stately facade
of Stephenson's
railway station has
managed to escape
the fell hand of
developers. Long
may it remain.

THE BEACH, RUSWARP AND SANDSEND

THE SANDS *1923* 74305

At this date, the old fashioned, rather cumbersome bathing machines were being replaced by bathing tents, the forerunners of the wooden huts which came later. The attendant facilitated the drying of bathing towels (foreground). The donkeys patiently await custom (right).

THE SANDS *1923* 74306

As soon as the tide recedes the pierrots erect their stage and start their performance. There was no charge for watching from the sidelines, though the deckchairs were for hire and someone went round with the collection box.

THE SANDS
1927 80175

Beside Beach Villa with the Metropole just behind, the new cliff lift was in process of being constructed; it was eventually to make access to and from the beach much simpler. Having dug their sand castle, the children in the foreground are now collecting seawater for its moat.

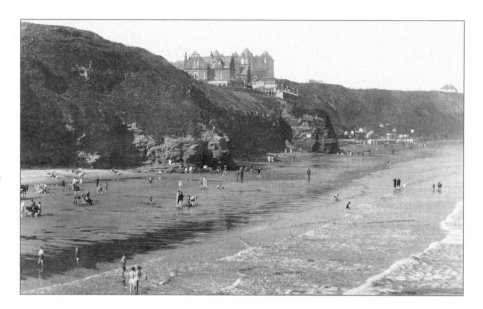

THE SANDS *1927* 80176

As of yore, the bathing towels are drying (left). Beyond, a couple of bell tents at the base of the cliff probably means that some hardy souls are camping there. White Point Hotel is on the skyline.

THE SANDS
1927 80179

The lifeguard keeps a careful eye on the party of swimmers, whilst another crowd gathers around the Punch and Judy show (centre left). Sand castles abound, and some even have channels dug for the seawater to find its way to the moats. The donkeys are not without willing customers.

THE BEACH *1955* W81135

The civil engineers of the future concentrate on their construction work, while a budding mountaineer attempts a climb of the stone wall (left). The cafes are in full swing, and the Battery Snack Bar (centre) offers 'Trays for the Sands'.

RUSWARP
The Bridge 1881
14491

Old documents relating to Whitby refer to the western part of the town as Ruswarp, though the village itself lies about a mile from the town. This picture shows the old road bridge, which was washed away in disastrous floods in the 1920s; the railway bridge is to its left. Ruswarp station is the first stop on the Whitby to Middlesbrough railway line – mercifully ignored by Beeching, much to the benefit of the many isolated villages lying in the Esk valley.

RUSWARP, *The Esk 1913* 66299

Several other British rivers bear the same name as Whitby's river. It is here that the Esk meets Ruswarp Dam and ceases to be tidal. The old road to Sleights runs along beside it through green tunnels, and is well loved by walkers and rowing boat enthusiasts alike.

RUSWARP
High Street c1960
R74004

No fewer than four tobacco advertisements surround the diminutive post office, run at this date by P W Wood, while the Unicorn Inn - later to become the Bridge Inn - is in the centre of the picture. Ruswarp Mill, which used to grind grain, cattle food and fertiliser, was virtually destroyed by a catastrophic fire in the 1900s.

RUSWARP, *The Bridge and the Church 1960* R74013

The new road bridge was built by the renowned engineering firm of Dorman Long of Middlesbrough, who also built the Sydney Harbour bridge. They made sure that this one would not be swept away by floods. St Bartholomew's Church is Victorian; its tower and spire are 120 feet high.

▼ **RIGG MILL** *1885* 18177

For generations this was a favourite destination for an afternoon's walk. Visitors could watch the water-driven wheel turning whilst they partook of refreshments. The wedding of the miller's daughter was a memorable occasion in the 1930s; the mill itself was decorated for the reception.

► **THE VIADUCT**
1884 18170

This massive memorial to the bricklayers' skill carried the LNER railway over the hilly terrain of this area in its journey from Teesside to Scarborough.

◄ **THE VIADUCT**
1884 18171

Although Beeching axed the trains on this line, he left this magnificent structure as it was. The rails have been removed, and a pleasant cycle track has been installed. There is talk of bringing back the railway, but talk costs nothing. In days of old, Whitby produced its own coal gas, and the gas works can be seen below the bridge. Today we have natural gas laid on.

► **LARPOOL HALL**
1985 ZZZ02101
(Reproduced by kind permission of Whitby Archives)

Larpool Hall is a dignified Georgian mansion dating from 1796. This was the home of the Turton family. After the First World War it was occupied by the many orphans left by that war, who were cared for by the National Children's Home. It has since been made into apartments.

SANDSEND
The Village c1885
18190

Nestling in the shelter of Lythe Bank, the ancient village holds the homes of many of the men who worked in the alum industry and on local estates. Alum was a chemical used in tanning leather and in the dyeworks to fix the dye used in the weaving industry. It was mined and extracted from local stone in the Whitby district, and provided much work for the miners. It became obsolete with the introduction of other chemicals. Today many of the dwellings in Sandsend are holiday cottages, much to the detriment of village life, since they stand empty for the greater part of the year.

▶ **SANDSEND**
The Village
1901 46807

The railway station is in the centre, to the left of the bridge. It was the final station along the scenic route from Teesside to Whitby. The railway line was axed during the Beeching era, and the sturdy bridge was lost at that time. The picture shows the extent of the small village.

◀**SANDSEND**
Kettleness Point
1925 78987

The old slipway remains, but today the cottages have been replaced by a car park. Notice the inundations made by previous centuries of alum mining and their spoil heaps on the point; these are now covered with vegetation.

▲ **SALTWICK BAY,** *Black Nab 1913* 66297

Just south of the abbey's cliffs lie these rocks, which show the inroads made by the alum mining industry during the previous centuries. Before the chemists discovered a simpler method of fixing the dyes used in cloth manufacturing, alum was successfully used for this purpose. It had first to be extracted from rich mineral-bearing stone. This was mined locally both at Saltwick and Sandsend, and provided welcome employment for the local menfolk. The seams have been exhausted, and the cliffs remain a favourite haunt of seabirds.

◄**SANDSEND**
The Beach 1925
78993

The railway line continues past the houses and the stone bridge of East Row, whilst the flow from the beck makes a tempting paddling pool. Bathing machines were still in use at this time, as we see on the right.

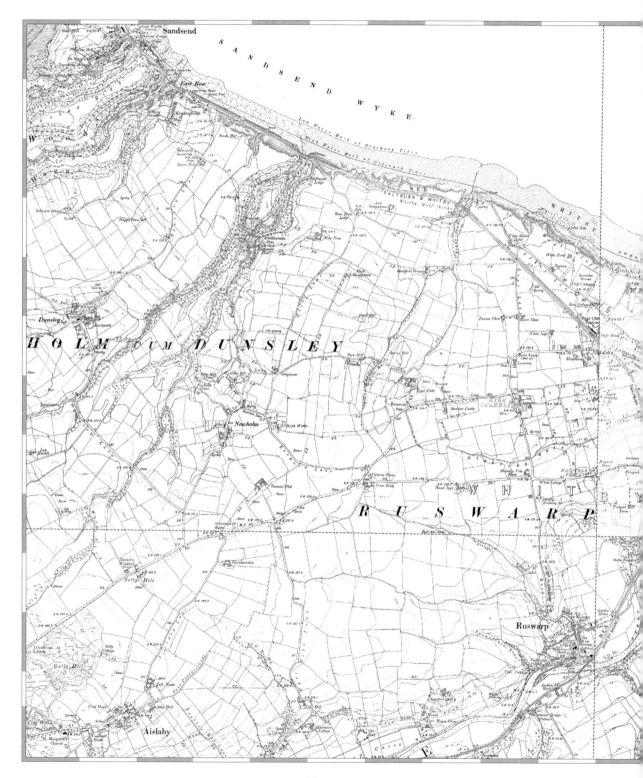

YORKSHIRE COUNTY MAP *showing Whitby and surrounding areas c1850 (section)*

INDEX

NAMES OF PRE-PUBLICATION BUYERS

THE FOLLOWING PEOPLE HAVE KINDLY SUPPORTED THIS BOOK BY
SUBSCRIBING TO COPIES BEFORE PUBLICATION.

Geoff Mohammed & Pauline Alderson
James Marlborough Allen
Miss Alexandra Louise Allison
In memory of Marian Gillian Allison
For my brother Ian Allport from Judith
Mr A S & Mrs P M Anderson, Lealholm, Whitby
Mr Stanley Anderson, Whitby
To Andy from Dorothy, Whitby 2005
Arches Guesthouse, West Cliff, Whitby
Malcolm G Barker, OBE
R A Barker & Family, Whitby
Mr & Mrs T W Barrowcliffe, Barnet
Barry & Ellen
Mary Bell & Family, Whitby
Angela Bennie, In memory of Mam Olivewood
Bill & Margaret, 31 years married, 2005
Mr S Boocock & Mrs J Boocock
Mr & Mrs K Bradburn, In memory of Justin
Arthur Broadley Jnr
In memory of Arthur Ernest Broadley 1919-76
In memory of Lily Broadley 1921-95
Captain & Mrs E Bryan
Mrs Else Bryan, In memory of Frank
Gary M Buck, Whitby
Joyce & Richard H Buck, Whitby
N Burnett
Graeme & Judy Burton, Guisborough
David M Carden
'Happy Birthday Carl' love Mum & Dad 2005
Mike & Linda Carthy, Yarm
Kenneth Cass
In memory of Milly & Les Chapman, Whitby
'Happy Birthday Chris', love Mum & Dad 2005
Mr D Clark & S A Clark, Whitby
Rev J & Anne Cooper 12/05/05
Mr & Mrs G Coulson, 'On our Anniversary'
Leslie Hicks Craig, Staithes, N. Yorkshire
Lord & Lady Crampton, Scotland
David Cross, Estbek House, Sandsend
To David & Maureen, love Mum & Dad
The Deacon Family
Paul & Lynn Dews from West Yorkshire

Sheila & the late Fred Dews, Wakefield
Luke Dickinson & Faye Dickinson, Whitby
Helen Dobson, Hutton Rudby
John Addison Dobson
Mr & Mrs P C Dodd
Phillip Dowson & Pam Skinner, Whitby
Mr E G & Mrs A Easton, Whitby
John Ellis, Leeds
Lord Ellis of Grindon
'Happy Birthday Ian Esson', love Lisa
Christopher Evans & Family, Cleator Moor
Jonathan Evans & Family, Fylingthorpe
Peggy Evans & Family, Whitby
Sue Evans & Family, Whitby
Fairhaven Country House Hotel
Colin Fenby
Reginald Firth, Mayor of Whitby 1984-1985
Mr R & Mrs M Fishlock, Loftus
David S Fox, Leeds
Polly Fraser
In memory of Annie Fryer, Esk Terrace
Peter & Sandra, The Gallery Guest House
B & J Gibbon & Family, Whitby
Wayne & Debbie Gibson, Whitby
Joan & Robert Gildroy, Whitby
The Goldsmith & Wrights, Livia Honey born
    09/11/04
Dennis & Moira Goodall
Ian & Sue Goodall
Mr T C Goodall & Mrs J E Goodall
In memory of Geoffrey & Ethel Graham
'Happy Birthday Graham' love Mam xxx
Susan Graham, Whitby
Roy & Heather Gray, Whitby
The Guy & Smith Families, Whitby
In memory of Mona & William Hardy, Whitby
In tribute to my husband, Alan R Harland
Richard & Cathy Harland 23/07/05
Dennis C Harrabin, Birmingham
Joseph J Harrison
Robert Hart, Hinderwell
Barbara Ann Hebbron

Mr A C Henderson & Mrs A M Henderson
The Henderson Family, Whitby
Ken & Marg Hewison 1955-2005, 50th Wedding
    Anniversary
In memory of Charles Vincent Hewlson, Whitby
The Hill Family, Pier Road, Whitby
Avis Mary Hodgson (nee Hewison & Jefferson)
The Hodgson Family, Tranmire
L E Hodgson, Whitby
To Brenda Hogan from all at Whitby
Sue & Alan Holmes, Middlesbrough
Joan Howard and son Richard of Stainsacre
To Rhiannon & Simon Howard, Whitby area
W J Howard, J.P, Catterick Garrison, Richmond
Christopher M Hugill
Keith Hunter, Whitby
'In memory of loved ones', Nora Hutchinson
To Colin W Hutton
To Ingrid, love Mum & Dad 2005
Mr Kenneth Jackson, Whitby
Jeff from Margaret
Martin G R Jenkins
The Johnson Family, Grosmont, North Yorks
J D Jones, Nottingham
In memory of Ken who loved Whitby
Kevin, 'my partner in life', love Maureen
B & E Kilpatrick, Whitby
Jack Knaggs, 70 on July 13th 2005
The Langley Family, Living the Dream!
Mr C I & Mrs A C Leach, Whitby
Mike Lee & Bev Milner who love Whitby
George & Eva Little
Nigel & Pat Little, Serenity 2005
In memory of George A Locker, Whitby xx
Mr T E & Mrs A Locker
Thomas H & Mary Locker, Whitby
To our parents, Freda & Peter Lofthouse
Sue Lonsdale & Geoff Jobling
Mr J Loughran, Leeds
Jack Lowther
Richard & Susan Macey
Mr A P & Mrs G Maher, Whitby
Jim Mandeville
To Louise Marot & David Fitzgerald
Martin Dale Marot & Lucy Marot, Whitby
Miss Julie A Marsay, Guisborough
The Mason Family, Whitby
Elisabeth Matthews 1935-2005
The Maxfield Family, Raw, Whitby

Marjorie Merifield
The Miller Family, Loftus, Cleveland
'Happy Days' Mom love Mickie xx
The Moon & Mussard Families, Whitby
In memory of John Redvers Moore, Egton
Annette & Edna Morrell
The Morrison Family
To a special Dad, Tom Morrison, Loftus
Mr & Mrs D Morton & Family of Whitby
Happy Birthday Mum, love Helen & Janet
To Mum with love, Oliver, Tanya, Toby & Tessa
To Mum with love from Pam & Mike xx
Uncle Nobby, Nottingham
Ronald & Joan Noble, Sleights
Grant & Hayley Norris, Glaisdale
Peter Osborne, Whitby Postman 1959 to 1994
In memory of John (Jack) Overend, Leeds
Baron Owen, Sleights Hall 2005
B Parkes
W H Parkin
William Parkin & Mary Parkin
Alison & Joseph Parzych on their Wedding
    25/06/05
For Pearl on her birthday, from Mark
To Peter & Joan, love Mum & Dad
Happy 60th Birthday Peter, love Pat & Nigel,
    Serenity 2005
Mr & Mrs D F Pomroy, Whitby
Anne & Geoff Poole
Mr Alf Porritt Jnr, born Ruswarp 14/12/26
Lavinia & Tony Pringle
John B Prudom, 'Forever a Whitby Lad'
Derek Puckrin, Landlord, 'First In Last Out'
Ian W Purves, Ruswarp
Mr S R & Mrs P R Purves, Yeovil
John & Jean Leyland Quarmby
The Raistrick Family, Whitby
To Ray with all my love, Gwen
Frank Readman, 'Tatie Market', Church Street
In memory of Jennie & Gordon Readman
To Ricky, 'Memories of home', from your Mum
The Rigg Family
Shirley Rigg, 'Loving Wife, Mother and
    Grandma'
As a tribute to my parents,
    Mrs & Mr A Robinson
Mr & Mrs C Robinson
The Robinson Family, Whitby
Mick & Di Robinson, Whitby

Ian Robson
Alison McKenzie Robson
To my parents, Mr & Mrs Roe, love Marie
George & Elaine Rollins, Whitby
Brian Rusling, York
The Russell Family, Whitby
To Annie Rymond, Staithes, on her birthday
For Jim & Dorothy Saunders, Whitby
Max & Sue Schietaert, Driffield
Geoffrey Scott
For Des Shaw on Father's Day, love Debbie & Stewart
In loving memory of Joe Shaw, Dad xx
For our Anniversary 2005, Mr & Mrs S Sheridan
The Frank Shipton Family, Whitby
Frank Shipton, 'Happy Birthday' Mam & Dad
Dr John Shorter, Whitby
In memory of Muriel Silson, Bramley, Leeds
Elsie Sinclair (nee Holtby), Ruswarp, Whitby
Rachel A Sleightholm
S Sleightholme, Whitby
Barbara Benson Smith, Whitby memories 1996-7
To the best Dad in the world, Mr Michael Smith
Steve, Andrea, Nicolle & Ryan Smith, Beverley
Barrie G Snoxell, Whitby
Mr G H Spark & Mrs J A Spark, Whitby
J J & J G Stanford, Hazel Head, Goatland
In memory of Albert Stanforth, Whitby
The Stokoe Family, Sleights, Whitby
Allan Stonehouse, Staithes
The Stonehouse Family, Redcar
Jean Stonehouse, Whitby
In memory of Raymond Storr, Whitby
William & Lisa Storr from Whitby
In memory of Mr William R Storr & Mrs Amy Storr
In memory of Don Stuart, Whitby
The Stuart Family, Whitby
Mr K G & Mrs S J Stuart, Whitby
Anthony Summerson
William Sutherland & Family
Sheila & Cyril Swales MBE 2005
To our parents, Evan & Irene Thomas
In memory of Stephen Glynn Thomas
The Eric Thompson & Doris Lyth Family
D A Tindale & M Tindale, 50th Wedding Anniversary
The Tindall Family, Stripes Farm, Hawsker, Whitby
In memory of 'Uncle Tom'

Mrs Freda Townley
Mrs Freda M & Mr T Havelock Turner
The Twigge Family, Robin Hood's Bay
Craig Tyreman, Whitby
Fred & Barbara Tyreman, Whitby
Philip & Janet Tyreman, Copmanthorpe
Vanessa & Derek, Whitby, North Yorkshire
Barbara Vaughan 1935-2005
To Pete & Eve Walker, love Pat & Nigel, Serenity 2005
In memory of Malcolm Waller, Whitby
To Simon, Jacob, Benjamin & Emily Walton
The Ward Family, Brotton
In memory of Jack Waters, Cobbler, Whitby
M N Watson, Egton Grange
In memory of Leslie Weatherill
John M Wedgwood, Robin Hood's Bay
Mrs Eleanor Weightman, Maghull
The Welford Family, Oak House Farm, Roxby
Mr J & Mrs K Wetherhill
A Wheatley
Col & Di Wheeldon, Burton-on-Trent
For our sons, Charlie and James Wheeldon, Whitby
Dorothy A Whelan, Whitby
From Wakefield, Anne & Richard Whiteman
John & Neil Whitley, Redcar, Yorks
The Williamson Family, Fylingthorpe
A Wilson, Whitby
The Wilson Family, Whitby
Geoff, Ann & Lee Wilson, Whitby
Paul Wilson, Birch Avenue, Sleights
Maurice Winspear, Redcar
For Margaret (Peggy) Wood
Andy Worth, Hawsker
Mr & Mrs David Wright
Mr H W Young & Mrs A M Young, Skelton
A C Young, Whitby

FREE PRINT OF YOUR CHOICE

Mounted Print
Overall size 14 x 11 inches (355 x 280mm)

Choose any Frith photograph in this book.
Simply complete the Voucher opposite and
return it with your remittance for £2.25 (to cover
postage and handling) and we will print the
photograph of your choice in SEPIA (size 11 x 8
inches) and supply it in a cream mount with a
burgundy rule line (overall size 14 x 11 inches).
**Please note: photographs with a reference
number starting with a "Z" are not Frith
photographs and cannot be supplied under
this offer.**
Offer valid for delivery to one UK address only.

PLUS: **Order additional Mounted Prints
at HALF PRICE - £7.49 each** (normally £14.99)
If you would like to order more Frith prints from
this book, possibly as gifts for friends and family,
you can buy them at half price (with no
additional postage and handling costs).

PLUS: **Have your Mounted Prints framed**
For an extra £14.95 per print you can have your
mounted print(s) framed in an elegant polished
wood and gilt moulding, overall size 16 x
13 inches (no additional postage and handling
required).

IMPORTANT!

**These special prices are only available if you use
this form to order . You must use the ORIGINAL
VOUCHER on this page (no copies permitted). We
can only despatch to one UK address. This offer
cannot be combined with any other offer.**

Send completed Voucher form to:
**The Francis Frith Collection, Frith's Barn,
Teffont, Salisbury, Wiltshire SP3 5QP**

CHOOSE A PHOTOGRAPH FROM THIS BOOK

Voucher for **FREE** and Reduced Price *Frith Prints*

*Please do not photocopy this voucher. Only the original is valid,
so please fill it in, cut it out and return it to us with your order.*

Picture ref no	Page no	Qty	Mounted @ £7.49	Framed + £14.95	Total Cost £
		1	Free of charge*	£	£
			£7.49	£	£
			£7.49	£	£
			£7.49	£	£
			£7.49	£	£
			£7.49	£	£

*Please allow 28 days
for delivery.
Offer available to one
UK address only*

* Post & handling	£2.25
Total Order Cost	£

Title of this book . . . .

I enclose a cheque/postal order for £ . . . .

made payable to 'The Francis Frith Collection'

OR please debit my Mastercard / Visa / Maestro / Amex
card, details below

Card Number

Issue No (Maestro only)   Valid from (Maestro)

Expires   Signature

Name Mr/Mrs/Ms . . . .

Address . . . .

. . . .

. . . .

. . . . Postcode . . . .

Daytime Tel No . . . .

Email . . . .

ISBN 1-85937-491-3   Valid to 31/12/07

Would you like to find out more about Francis Frith?

We have recently recruited some entertaining speakers who are happy to visit local groups, clubs and societies to give an illustrated talk documenting Frith's travels and photographs. If you are a member of such a group and are interested in hosting a presentation, we would love to hear from you.

Our speakers bring with them a small selection of our local town and county books, together with sample prints. They are happy to take orders. A small proportion of the order value is donated to the group who have hosted the presentation. The talks are therefore an excellent way of fundraising for small groups and societies.

Can you help us with information about any of the Frith photographs in this book?

We are gradually compiling an historical record for each of the photographs in the Frith archive. It is always fascinating to find out the names of the people shown in the pictures, as well as insights into the shops, buildings and other features depicted.

If you recognize anyone in the photographs in this book, or if you have information not already included in the author's caption, do let us know. We would love to hear from you, and will try to publish it in future books or articles.

Our production team

Frith books are produced by a small dedicated team at offices in the converted Grade II listed 18th-century barn at Teffont near Salisbury, illustrated above. Most have worked with the Frith Collection for many years. All have in common one quality: they have a passion for the Frith Collection. The team is constantly expanding, but currently includes:

Paul Baron, Phillip Brennan, Jason Buck, John Buck, Ruth Butler, Heather Crisp, David Davies, Louis du Mont, Isobel Hall, Lucy Hart, Julian Hight, Peter Horne, James Kinnear, Karen Kinnear, Tina Leary, Stuart Login, David Marsh, Lesley-Ann Millard, Sue Molloy, Glenda Morgan, Wayne Morgan, Sarah Roberts, Kate Rotondetto, Dean Scource, Eliza Sackett, Terence Sackett, Sandra Sampson, Adrian Sanders, Sandra Sanger, Julia Skinner, Miles Smith, Lewis Taylor, Shelley Tolcher, Lorraine Tuck, David Turner, Amanita Wainwright and Ricky Williams.